CHARLEY HARPER'S
sticky critters · VOLUME 2

Animals in America's National Parks · A Sticker Kit

Over 190 reusable vinyl stickers!

Welcome to
Sticky Critters Volume 2

The 12 animals depicted in this kit all live in America's national parks. You can make each of them from the included stickers, which are based on artwork by Charley Harper (American, 1922–2007).

Use the board that came in the box as your play area—press the stickers onto the board and move them around as you like. To keep the stickers safe, remember to put them back on their sticker sheets when you're finished playing with them.

How do the sticker animals look to you? Happy? Shy? Grumpy? Curious? Fierce? Friendly? Harper studied wildlife characteristics while developing an eye for their colors, shapes, patterns, and textures. A lifelong conservationist, he was commissioned to design posters for the National Park Service and other organizations.

Have fun sticking and re-sticking Harper's clever critters. Like the artist, perhaps you will want to learn more about these and other animals that inhabit America's national parks.

Happy stickering!

I am a mountain lion.

Thanks to my big paws and strong legs, I am a great swimmer.
But like many cats, I don't really like to get wet.

I am a raccoon.

As an adult, I wear a "mask" and have rings on my tail. When I was a youngster, known as a *kit*, I did not yet have these markings.

I am a red fox.

I am an omnivore. I eat everything from birds to berries.

I am a great horned owl.

I am a ferocious hunter. I catch and eat so many skunks that both my nest and I start to smell skunky.

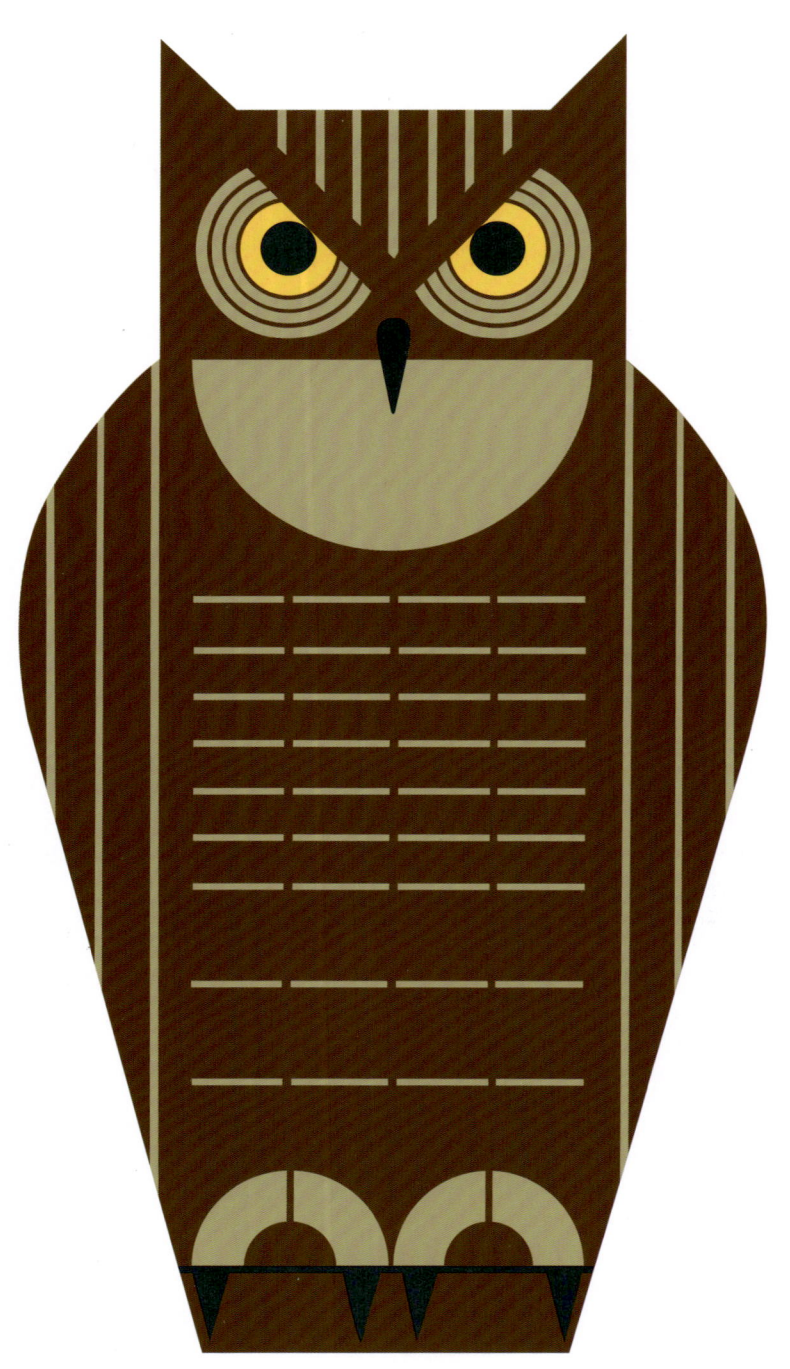

I am a ground squirrel.

I am also a homebody. I rarely venture far from the entrance to my cozy burrow.

I am an opossum.

When scared, I "play dead" to fool predators. After the danger passes, I get up and go on my way.

I am a cottontail rabbit.

My fluffy white tail isn't just cute; it confuses animals that are chasing me.

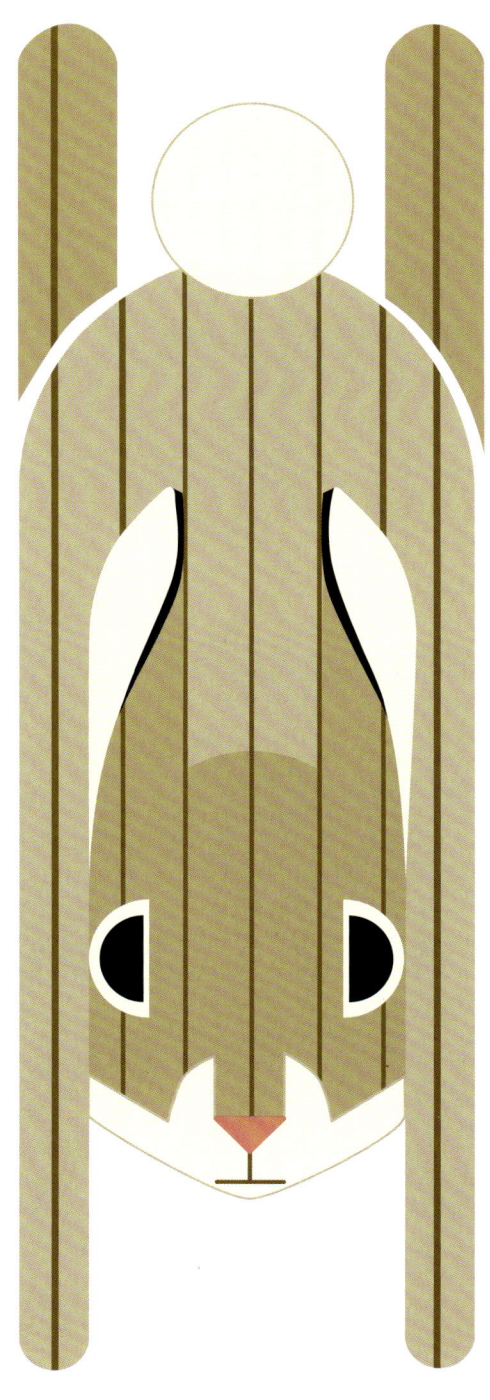

I am a black bear.

Don't feed me! But I do enjoy munching
on berries that I find in the wild.

I am a deer.

As a fawn, I have spots on my fur, but these will disappear when I grow into my adult coat.

I am a bobcat.

I have tufted ears and a ruff of fur on my cheeks.
I got my name from my stubby tail.

I am a marmot.

I am an awesome digger. My burrow has a
main entrance and an escape tunnel.

I am a gray wolf.

I like to sing alone or in a chorus with a few of my pack mates. My howls can be heard up to six miles away.

mountain lion

raccoon

red fox

great horned owl

ground squirrel

opossum

cottontail rabbit

black bear

deer

bobcat

marmot

gray wolf

PomegranateKids®, an imprint of
Pomegranate Communications, Inc.
105 SE 18th Ave., Portland, OR 97214
800-227-1428   pomegranate.com

This product is in compliance with the CPSIA. A General Conformity
Certificate and tracking information are available through Pomegranate.

Manufactured and Distributed by Pomegranate Communications, Inc.

Item No. AA949

Designed by Stephanie Odeh

Printed in China

ISBN 978-0-7649-7472-4